THE 1960S

Elizabeth
1960s

Maria
1960s

1965
One-shouldered maillot

1961
Bikini-style bathing suit

PLATE 1

1961
Bikini-style bathing suit

1965
One-shouldered maillot

Maria

1961
Nina Ricci (Crahay)
Silk ensemble

Elizabeth

1960
Yves Saint Laurent
Transparent chiffon dress

1960
Yves Saint Laurent
Transparent chiffon dress

1961
Nina Ricci (Crahay)
Silk ensemble

PLATE 6

THE 1960s

1961
Jacques Griffe
Linen suit

1961
Irene Galitzine
Crepe jacket and sheath

PLATE 7

Maria

1961
Irene Galitzine
Crepe jacket and sheath

Elizabeth

1961
Jacques Griffe
Linen suit

Maria

1962
Capucci
Chiffon cape-and-sheath outfit

Elizabeth

1962
Pierre Balmain
Evening gown

THE 1960S

1962
Pierre Balmain
Evening gown

1962
Capucci
Chiffon cape-and-sheath outfit

PLATE 8

THE 1960s

1962
Courrèges
Nine-tenths coat

1963
Givenchy
Tweed sport suit

PLATE 9

Maria

1963
Givenchy
Tweed sport suit

Elizabeth

1962
Courrèges
Nine-tenths coat

Maria

1963
Yves Saint Laurent
Organdy outfit

Elizabeth

1963
Jean Patou
Organdy gown

THE 1960s

1963
Jean Patou
Organdy gown

1963
Yves Saint Laurent
Organdy outfit

PLATE 10

THE 1960s

Do not cut out white areas between arms and body.

1964
Chanel
Wool suit

1964
Larry Aldrich
Unwaisted crepe dress with stole
(Hat by Halston)

PLATE 11

Maria

1964
Larry Aldrich
Unwaisted crepe dress with stole
(Hat by Halston)

Elizabeth

1964
Chanel
Wool suit

Maria

1965
Yves Saint Laurent
Jersey day dress

Elizabeth

1964
Courrèges
Jersey pants and jacket

THE 1960s

1964
Courrèges
Jersey pants and jacket

1965
Yves Saint Laurent
Jersey day dress

PLATE 12

THE 1960s

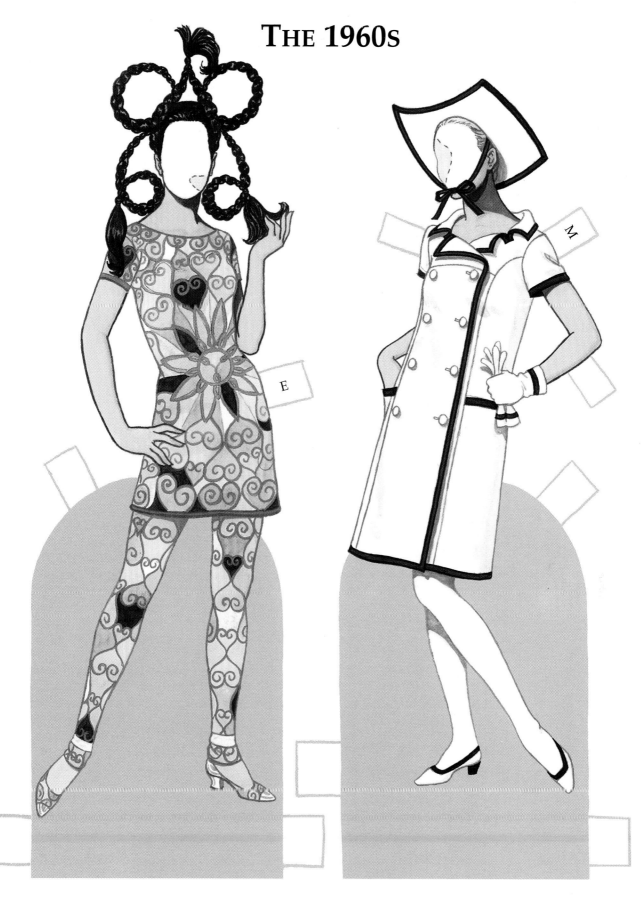

1965
Pucci
Minidress

1965
Courrèges
Wool coatdress

PLATE 13

Maria

1965
Courrèges
Wool coatdress

Elizabeth

1965
Pucci
Minidress

Maria

1966
Philippe Venet
Chiffon minidress

Elizabeth

1966
Paco Rabanne
Plastic dress

THE 1960s

1966
Paco Rabanne
Plastic dress

1966
Philippe Venet
Chiffon minidress

PLATE 14

THE 1960s

Do not cut out white areas between arms and body.

1966
Courrèges
Whipcord and organza jumpsuit

1967
Mary Quant
Wool minidress

PLATE 15

Maria

1967
Mary Quant
Wool minidress

Elizabeth

1966
Courrèges
Whipcord and organza jumpsuit

Maria

1967
Bill Blass
Crepe wedding dress

Elizabeth

1967
Rudi Gernreich
Silk dress

THE 1960S

Do not cut out
white area
between
arm and body.

1967
Rudi Gernreich
Silk dress

1967
Bill Blass
Crepe wedding dress

PLATE 16

THE 1960s

E

E

M

Do not cut out white areas between arms and body.

1968
Oscar de la Renta
Organdy overblouse and shorts

1968
Anne Fogarty
"Little Girl" dress

PLATE 17

Maria

1968
Anne Fogarty
"Little Girl" dress

Elizabeth

1968
Oscar de la Renta
Organdy overblouse and shorts

Maria

1969
Cardin
Wool coat, hooded sweater
and white skirt

Elizabeth

1968
Geoffrey Beene
Coatdress

THE 1960S

1968
Geoffrey Beene
Coatdress

1969
Cardin
Wool coat, hooded sweater
and white skirt

PLATE 18

Do not
cut out
white area
between arms
and body.

1969
Courrèges
Dress

1969
Yves Saint Laurent
Evening dress

PLATE 19

Maria

1969
Yves Saint Laurent
Evening dress

Elizabeth

1969
Courrèges
Dress

Debra

1970
House of Dior
Crepe-de-chine dress

Christine

1970
Zandra Rhodes
Quilted satin dress

1970
Zandra Rhodes
Quilted satin dress

1970
House of Dior
Crepe-de-chine dress

PLATE 20

THE 1970s

Do not cut out white area between arms and body.

1970
Yves Saint Laurent
Lamé dress

1971
Chloé
Wraparound skirt and shawl

PLATE 21

Debra

1971
Chloé
Wraparound skirt
and shawl

Christine

1970
Yves Saint Laurent
Lamé dress

Debra

1971
Tuffin and Foale
Checkerboard-print dress
and quilted trousers

Christine

1971
Biba
Wool pantsuit

THE **1970s**

C

D

1971
Biba
Wool pantsuit

1971
Tuffin and Foale
Checkerboard-print dress
and quilted trousers

PLATE 22

THE 1970s

1972
Bill Blass
Pleated skirt and
dropped-waist top

1972
Mary Quant
Two-piece dress

PLATE 23

Debra

1972
Mary Quant
Two-piece dress

Christine

1972
Bill Blass
Pleated skirt and
dropped-waist top

Debra

1973
Yves Saint Laurent
Cardigan, pleated skirt
and "see-through" blouse

Christine

1972
Horrockses
Cotton hostess dress

THE 1970s

Do not cut out white areas between arms and body.

C

D

1972
Horrockses
Cotton hostess dress

1973
Yves Saint Laurent
Cardigan, pleated skirt and
"see-through" blouse

PLATE 24

THE 1970s

1973
Ted Lapidus
Wool pantsuit

1973
Roland Klein
Silk-jersey gown

PLATE 25

Debra

1973
Roland Klein
Silk-jersey gown

Christine

1973
Ted Lapidus
Wool pantsuit

Debra

1974
Loris Azzare
Mousseline-de-soie gown

Christine

1974
Laug
Lamé top and
crepe-georgette skirt

THE 1970s

cut out; apply a thin line of glue to shaded area and glue to back of hairdo, forming a pocket to slip head into

Do not cut out white area between arm and body.

1974
Laug
Lamé top and
crepe-georgette skirt

1974
Loris Azzare
Mousseline-de-soie gown

PLATE 26

THE 1970S

1974
Sonia Rykiel
Cape, sweater and skirt

1975
Andre Peters
Cape, hat and scarf (trousers by
Wendy Dagworthy)

PLATE 27

Debra

1975
Andre Peters
Cape, hat and scarf
(trousers by Wendy
Dagworthy)

Christine

1974
Sonia Rykiel
Cape, sweater and skirt

Debra

1975
Laura Ashley
Pinafore, skirt, blouse
and apron

Christine

1975
John Bates
Duster

C

C

D

Do not cut out
white area
between arm
and body.

1975
John Bates
Duster

1975
Laura Ashley
Pinafore, skirt, blouse
and apron

PLATE 28

THE 1970S

1976
Halston
Shirtwaist dress and jacket

1976
Yves Saint Laurent
"Peasant-look" cape, blouse,
skirt and turban

PLATE 29

Debra

1976
Yves Saint Laurent
"Peasant-look" cape, blouse,
skirt and turban

Christine

1976
Halston
Shirtwaist dress
and jacket

Debra

1977
Sisan for Valentino
Coordinated blouse, skirt,
pants and scarf

Christine

1977
Hubert de Givenchy
Dinner dress with
detachable sleeves

THE **1970s**

Do not cut out white areas between arms and body.

1977
Hubert de Givenchy
Dinner dress with
detachable sleeves

1977
Sisan for Valentino
Coordinated blouse, skirt,
pants and scarf

PLATE 30

THE 1970s

C

D

1977
Kenzo
"Big Look" shirt and skirt

1978
Courrèges
Jacket, sweater, shirt
and trousers

PLATE 31

Debra

1978
Courrèges
Jacket, sweater, shirt
and trousers

Christine

1977
Kenzo
"Big Look" shirt and skirt

Debra

1978
Oscar de la Renta
Velvet dress
(brass belt by Tess Shalom)

Christine

1978
Yves Saint Laurent
Evening ensemble

THE 1970S

1978
Yves Saint Laurent
Evening ensemble

1978
Oscar de la Renta
Velvet dress
(brass belt by Tess Shalom)

PLATE 32

THE 1970S

Do not cut out
white areas between
arms and body.

1979
Thierry Mugler
Jumpsuit

1979
Claude Montana
Gabardine trench coat

PLATE 33

Debra

1979
Claude Montana
Gabardine trench coat

Christine

1979
Thierry Mugler
Jumpsuit

Debra

1979
Albert Caprero
Velvet-and-silk
evening gown

Christine

1979
Ralph Lauren
Silk smoking jacket

THE 1970s

Do not cut out white areas between arms and body.

1979
Ralph Lauren
Silk smoking jacket

1979
Albert Caprero
Velvet-and-silk
evening gown

PLATE 34

THE 1980s

1980
Betty Hanson and Company
Shirtwaist dress and short jacket

1980
Missoni
Jacket, hat, and skirt

PLATE 35

Laura

1980
Missoni
Jacket, hat, and skirt

Angela

1980
Betty Hanson and
Company
Shirtwaist dress and
short jacket

Laura

1980
Halston
Classic sheath and
box coat

Angela

1980
Claude Montana
Cotton dress

THE 1980s

1980
Claude Montana
Cotton dress

1980
Halston
Classic sheath and box coat

PLATE 36

THE 1980S

1981
Perry Ellis
Tank top with skirt, petticoats,
knit cap and stockings

1981
Calvin Klein
Metallic print dress with
knee-high leather boots

PLATE 37

Laura

1981
Calvin Klein
Metallic print dress with
knee-high leather boots

Angela

1981
Perry Ellis
Tank top with skirt,
petticoats, knit cap
and stockings

Laura

1982
Marc Bohan for
House of Dior
Suit

Angela

1982
Giorgio Armani
Blouse with cut-off pants

1982
Giorgio Armani
Blouse with cut-off pants

1982
Marc Bohan for
House of Dior
Suit

PLATE 38

THE 1980s

Cut out shape above and glue edge to back of hat to form a pocket; let dry. Slip doll's head into pocket.

1982
Kasper
Silk "tee" shirt and skirt

1983
Bernard Perris
Flannel suit

PLATE 39

Laura

1983
Bernard Perris
Flannel suit

Angela

1982
Kasper
Silk "tee" shirt and skirt

Laura

1983
Karl Lagerfeld for the
House of Chloé
Dress with beads
and sequins

Angela

1983
Carolina Herrera
Organza gown

THE 1980s

1983
Carolina Herrera
Organza gown

1983
Karl Lagerfeld for the
House of Chloé
Dress with beads and sequins

PLATE 40

THE 1980s

1984
Bill Blass
Evening gown

1984
Valentino
Silk sheath

PLATE 41

Laura

1984
Valentino
Silk sheath

Angela

1984
Bill Blass
Evening gown

Laura

1985
Jacqueline de Ribes
Silk crepe dress

Angela

1984
Norma Kamali
Fleece topcoat, slacks,
scarf, and brimmed hat

THE 1980s

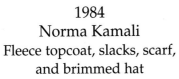

1984
Norma Kamali
Fleece topcoat, slacks, scarf,
and brimmed hat

1985
Jacqueline de Ribes
Silk crepe dress

PLATE 42

THE 1980s

1985
Donna Karan
Suede jacket, wool jersey skirt
and suede boots

1985
Gianfranco Ferré
Suede jacket over slacks

PLATE 43

Laura

1985
Gianfranco Ferré
Suede jacket over slacks

Angela

1985
Donna Karan
Suede jacket, wool jersey
skirtand suede boots

Laura

1986
Adolfo
Dress with a full-length
zipper

Angela

1986
Anne Klein
Sweater dress with patent
leather belt

THE 1980s

1986
Anne Klein
Sweater dress with patent
leather belt

1986
Adolfo
Dress with a full-length
zipper

PLATE 44

THE 1980s

1986
Krizia
Ribbed cashmere and mohair
sweater dress and coat

1987
Yves Saint Laurent
Silk crepe evening dress

PLATE 45

Laura

1987
Yves Saint Laurent
Silk crepe evening dress

Angela

1986
Krizia
Ribbed cashmere and
mohair sweater dress
and coat

Laura

1987
Oscar de la Renta
Short dress

Angela

1987
Geoffrey Beene
Lace confection

THE 1980s

1987
Geoffrey Beene
Lace confection

1987
Oscar de la Renta
Short dress

PLATE 46

THE 1980s

1988
Arnold Scaasi
Evening gown with a velvet bodice
and satin skirt

1988
Emanuel Ungaro
Strapless dress with dropped
waist and short skirt

PLATE 47

Laura

1988
Emanuel Ungaro
Strapless dress with
dropped waist and short
skirt

Angela

1988
Arnold Scaasi
Evening gown with a velvet bodice
and satin skirt

Laura

1988
Carolyn Roehm
Wool crepe dress with
bolero jacket

Angela

1988
Lacroix
Wool suit with
mink facing

THE 1980s

1988
Lacroix
Wool suit with mink facing

1988
Carolyn Roehm
Wool crepe dress with
bolero jacket

PLATE 48

THE 1980s

1989
Givenchy
Tailored sheath with
a full-length cape

1989
Bob Mackie
Gown in chiffon over silk,
with a sequin-studded jacket

PLATE 49

Laura

1989
Bob Mackie
Gown in chiffon over
silk, with a
sequin-studded jacket

Angela

1989
Givenchy
Tailored sheath with
a full-length cape

Nicole

1990
Christian Lacroix
Patterned silk ensemble

Jennifer

1990
Emanuel Ungaro
Lamé evening gown

1990
Emanuel Ungaro
Lamé evening gown

1990
Christian Lacroix
Patterned silk ensemble

PLATE 50

THE 1990s

1990
Geoffrey Beene
Silk jacquard evening
ensemble

1991
Oscar de la Renta
Silk shantung dress
and coat

PLATE 51

Nicole

1991
Oscar de la Renta
Silk shantung dress
and coat

Jennifer

1990
Geoffrey Beene
Silk jacquard evening
ensemble

Nicole

1991
Todd Oldham
Patchwork plaid suit

Jennifer

1991
Valentino
Bell skirted evening
ensemble

THE 1990S

1991
Valentino
Bell-skirted evening
ensemble

1991
Todd Oldham
Patchwork plaid suit

PLATE 52

Do not cut out
white areas
between arms
and body.

1992
Arnold Scaasi
Polka dot strapless
crepe dress

1992
Michael Kors
Short strapless dress
and cardigan

PLATE 53

Nicole

1992
Michael Kors
Short strapless dress
and cardigan

Jennifer

1992
Arnold Scaasi
Polka dot strapless
crepe dress

Nicole

1993
Bill Blass
Knit tube dress

Jennifer

1992
Bob Mackie
Velvet and taffeta
evening gown

THE 1990s

Do not cut out white areas between arms and body.

1992
Bob Mackie
Velvet and taffeta
evening gown

1993
Bill Blass
Knit tube dress

PLATE 54

1993
Linda Allard for
Ellen Tracy
Pin-stripe suit

1993
Adolfo
Polka-dot print ensemble

PLATE 55

Nicole

1993
Adolfo
Polka-dot print
ensemble

Jennifer

1993
Linda Allard for
Ellen Tracy
Pin-stripe suit

Nicole

1994
Louis Féraud
Evening gown with
capelike collar

Jennifer

1994
Nina Ricci
Pleated silk gown

THE 1990s

Do not cut out white area between arm and body.

1994
Nina Ricci
Pleated silk gown

1994
Louis Féraud
Evening gown with
capelike collar

PLATE 56

THE 1990s

1994
Jean-Louis Scherrer
Minidress ball gown

1995
Gianfranco Ferré
Classic suit and topcoat

PLATE 57

Nicole

1995
Gianfranco Ferré
Classic suit and topcoat

Jennifer

1994
Jean-Louis Scherrer
Minidress ball gown

Nicole

1995
Vera Wang
Corset-bodice ball gown

Jennifer

1995
Thierry Mugler
Miniskirted suit and
vinyl pants

THE 1990s

1995
Thierry Mugler
Miniskirted suit and
vinyl pants

1995
Vera Wang
Corset-bodice ball gown

Do not cut out
white areas
between arms
and body.

PLATE 58

THE 1990S

PLATE 59

1996
Carolina Herrera
Satin wedding suit

1996
Donna Karan
Body-hugging silk knit
tube dress

Nicole

1996
Donna Karan
Body-hugging silk knit
tube dress

Jennifer

1996
Carolina Herrera
Satin wedding suit

Nicole

1997
Isaac Mizrahi
Plunging-neckline
tailored suit

Jennifer

1996
Norma Kamali
Panne velvet
lamb-trimmed ensemble

1996
Norma Kamali
Panne velvet
lamb-trimmed ensemble

1997
Isaac Mizrahi
Plunging-neckline
tailored suit

PLATE 60

THE 1990S

1997
Giorgio Armani
Unstructured great coat
and full-cut pants

1997
Gianni Versace
Slinky silk knit
evening gown

PLATE 61

Nicole

1997
Gianni Versace
Slinky silk knit
evening gown

Jennifer

1997
Giorgio Armani
Unstructured great coat
and full-cut pants

Nicole

1998
Karl Lagerfeld for
Chanel
Sequined tulle dress

Jennifer

1998
John Galliano for Dior
"Scheherazade"
kimono and gown

THE 1990s

1998
John Galliano for Dior
"Scheherazade" kimono
and gown

1998
Karl Lagerfeld for
Chanel
Sequined tulle dress

PLATE 62

The 1990s

1998
Alexander McQueen for
Givenchy
Wool coat with gray fox collar

1999
Ralph Lauren
Cashmere sweater with
satin ball skirt

PLATE 63

Nicole

1999
Ralph Lauren
Cashmere sweater with
satin ball skirt

Jennifer

1998
Alexander McQueen
for Givenchy
Wool coat with
gray fox collar

Nicole

1999
Jean Paul Gaultier
Ostrich-trimmed silk gown
with ostrich fan

Jennifer

1999
Dolce & Gabbana
Beaded
lace-embroidered dress

1999
Dolce & Gabbana
Beaded
lace-embroidered dress

1999
Jean Paul Gaultier
Ostrich-trimmed silk gown
with ostrich fan

PLATE 64

FASHIONS OF FOUR DECADES

THE 1960s

In 1960, the reins of the high-fashion industry were still in the hands of French couturiers such as Yves Saint Laurent (for the House of Dior) and Balenciaga. But change was in the wind. During the fifties fashion had begun to go international, notable designers from Italy, Spain, Ireland, and America having made incursions into what had been a Parisian monopoly. Almost singlehandedly, Mary Quant, a young Englishwoman, wrested the dictates of fashion from the Parisian designers and revolutionized the entire industry when she began to design clothes specifically for the teenager. Her clothes were notable for their bright, bold colors, short miniskirts, colorful tights in lieu of stockings and "kooky" accessories, such as thigh-high boots, wide belts and outsized shoulder bags. Her clothes were all ready-to wear and inexpensive, leading to the concept of "throw-away" fashion. By the mid-sixties her fashion had crystallized the youth cult and had made "Swinging London" the leading center for new women's fashions. For the first time in fashion history, the designers had to cope with the reality that fashion would no longer be dictated by the elite wealthy class; the big bucks now lay in young middle- and working-class consumers who wanted comfort and flash in their ready-made clothing.

Two young Parisian designers, Courrèges and Cardin, were among the first to recognize the power of this youth cult and to formulate it as couturier fashion. Courrèges was able to corral the trends of the iconoclastic youth cult into a more formalized high fashion and was the first of the Parisian designers to raise skirts to the rarefied heights of the mini. His clothes were noted for their structured, austere, sculptured look. Cardin's contribution to the fashions of the sixties was an almost architectural look, with a clean, severe line and geometric shapes.

By the mid-sixties, the rule in fashion design was to break the rules. The most important fashion trend was the shortness of the skirt to the hip and the emphasis of the leg and novelty tights. By 1967, all designer collections seemed to feature unisex clothing—a misnomer in that it promoted women's clothing that was mannish, but did not dare to encourage men to wear dresses, although the shoulder bag was promoted as an accessory and the use of cologne and jewelry became more popular.

During the entire decade, Yves Saint Laurent was one of the decade's leading iconoclasts. Among his contributions were Pop Art fashions, see-through dresses and blouses designed to be worn over nothing at all, Mondrian-inspired geometric sheath dresses and, by the end of the decade, the introduction of the "maxi" or long skirt.

Throughout the sixties the trend was toward a more experimental, inventive, and childlike appearance veneering a foundation of blatant sexuality. Couturier collections diminished to small private affairs, the emphasis shifting to the ready-to-wear business.

THE 1970s

The emphasis on youth that had begun in the sixties continued into the seventies. The early seventies were a period of throwaway elegance, based on inexpensive and elaborate synthetic fabrics. There was an almost barbaric splendor in the use of silver and gold and lush textures and colors. A worldwide oil shortage beginning about 1973, and the consequent skyrocketing prices, would soon bring such extravagance to an end. At about the same time, awareness of the environmental problems of the world began to come to the fore. International concern about endangered species of animals made it socially unacceptable in many circles to wear exotic furs, and synthetic "fun" furs were promoted as an alternative.

Cheap travel and global communication suggested all sorts of exotic fashions from around the world. Mid-seventies fashion also mirrored contemporary history from space travel to Olympic events. Fabric texture or print was often substituted for cut, a trend encouraged by the explosion of designer ready-to-wear and the advent of the boutique. Saint Laurent was probably the leading designer of the decade, and led the pack in exploiting old films, exotic locations, and history to create looks for each season.

Fashion had passed from the haute couture to the mass market, a market dominated by the young who had money for clothing and few other commitments for their wages. Casual dressing became a big factor in fashion. Women were exhorted to "do their own thing," regardless of the consequences, with designers turning out fashions in deliberately bad taste. Nostalgia was a recurring theme throughout the decade, often tied into the blockbuster film of the season, as in the case of *The Great Gatsby* and the resulting revival of twenties' fashions. In 1975, the "Big Look" came into fashion, with the designer Kenzo stating, "Much too big is the right size."

The heyday of "Punk" was 1976 to 1978. Originally from the streets, punk fashions, with their rebellious, sado-masochistic overtones and concentration on the outrageous, were associated with underground music. Punk-rock stars sported black rubber dresses, oversize crosses, Nazi memorabilia, spike-heeled shoes and spiky hairdos, black leather corsetry, death-symbolism accessories and caked, geometric makeup. In response, fashion collections went black and bits and pieces of punk fashions were incorporated.

Middle Eastern and folk costume also became the inspiration for 1976 fashion, bringing tunics, turbans, capes, and hoods. By 1978, designers had turned the street look of punk into the "New Romanticism" with modern versions of ruffles, crinolines, flounces, ribbons and bows, deep décolleté, mock bustles, and leg-o'-mutton sleeves, all with a purposely disheveled look to the hair, heavy makeup and gaudy costume jewelry. By the end of the seventies there seemed to be no particular direction to fashion, each designer pursuing his or her own inspiration and offering his or her own look.

THE 1980s

The fashion designers of the eighties, like many of their predecessors of the late seventies, found inspiration in the designs of the past. The real news of this decade was in ease of wear and fit. Comfort became key; no longer would women be constricted and confined by structured foundation garments.

I

With the unusually cold winter weather of the early eighties came a drop in hemlines and a layering of outerwear. When winters warmed in the second half of the decade, skirt lengths rose and outerwear became lighter, too.

In fabrics, polyester was "out" and natural fabrics were "in." The type and style of fabric—luxury fabrics, novelty weaves, and prints—often became more important than the cut of the clothing.

During the eighties, the split widened between high fashion and mass fashion. Men and women who were obsessed with fitness and running inspired those less active to wear jogging suits, stretch bodysuits, gym shorts, tee shirts, and running shoes for leisure. While some women continued to choose dresses for office, cocktails, and evening wear, more and more women preferred the comfort and convenience of pants.

With the eighties came a great demand in the mass market for "designer label ready-to-wear." As a result, more clothing designers rose to prominence during the eighties than in any previous decade.

THE 1990s

The fashions of the last decade of the twentieth century were as volatile as the weather. In the search for new styles, the fashion industry lurched from "modern" to "retro," from "grunge" to "glamour," from "glitz" to "minimalist" to "military," concluding in a flurry of sumptuous beaded, jeweled, and embroidered garments. The decade also was marked by mega-mergers of design houses and the blurring of product lines—for example, producers of luggage turned to fashion design to enter new markets. In an attempt to revitalize old couture houses, "hot" young designers hopped from house to house. To add to the confusion, some designers had their own label but also designed for another establishment, such as Michael Kors for Celine, John Galliano for Dior, Alexander McQueen for Givenchy, and Marc Jacobs for Perry Ellis. By the end of the nineties, supermodels were losing ground as fashion oracles as they were replaced by rock stars and entertainment personalities.

ABOUT THE DESIGNS

PLATE 1. *Left:* 1965. One-shouldered maillot. *Right:* 1961. Bikini-style bathing suit.

PLATE 2. *Left:* 1977. Catalina swimwear with matching turban. *Right:* 1977. Maidenform's "Sweet Nothings" bikini underwear.

PLATE 3. *Left:* 1980. A bikini swimsuit of nylon spandex in blocks of color, by Jantzen. *Right:* 1980. The underwear, by Maidenform, features a deep plunging bra and matching bikini panties made of nylon Quiana with eyelet trim. By the eighties, swimsuits and underwear were often cut the same way; the principal difference was in the weight and sheerness of the fabrics.

PLATE 4. *Left:* 1998. A shoulder-baring swimsuit of silver metallic stretch fabric from Anne Klein. *Right:* 1998. The model's soft cotton-knit undergarments are an Anne Cole design. Tank tops often were worn as outerwear or layered under the straps of an evening gown for a "grunge" look in the nineties.

PLATE 5. *Left:* 1960. House of Dior black-and-white silk print suit: straw beehive hat. *Right:* 1960. Jacques Heim cotton evening dress: full skirt ankle-length in front, floor-length in back; contrasting bow and band as ornamentation.

PLATE 6. *Left:* 1960. Yves Saint Laurent transparent chiffon dress: bands of beading; flesh-colored underwear. *Right:* 1961. Nina Ricci silk ensemble.

PLATE 7. *Left:* 1961. Jacques Griffe linen suit: straw flowerpot hat. *Right:* 1961. Irene Galitzine crepe jacket and sheath: bias-scarfed combing jacket; jeweled at the neckline.

PLATE 8. *Left:* 1962. Pierre Balmain evening gown: long, paneled dress reminiscent of the nineteenth century; the bodice embroidered with gold-and-coral paillettes; bare shoulders. *Right:* 1962. Capucci chiffon cape-and-sheath outfit: open-front cape with rounded back; severe casquelike hat.

PLATE 9. *Left:* 1962. Courrèges nine-tenths coat: leather hat. *Right:* 1963. Givenchy tweed sport suit.

PLATE 10. *Left:* 1963. Jean Patou organdy gown: embroidered, with appliquéd motifs. *Right:* 1963. Yves Saint Laurent organdy outfit: silk, with guipure lace.

PLATE 11. *Left:* 1964. Chanel nubby-weave suit: straight-cut skirt and hip-length box jacket; gardenia tops the straw hat. *Right:* 1964. Larry Aldrich unwaisted crepe dress with stole: kick-pleat flipping out at hem; Bianchini rayon crepe; straw hat.

PLATE 12. *Left:* 1964. Courrèges jersey pants and jacket: pants slit at ankle over leather boots; pearl-buttoned jacket; "waste basket" hat. *Right:* 1965. Yves Saint Laurent jersey day dress: patterning in the manner of Mondrian.

PLATE 13. *Left:* 1965. Pucci minidress: Pucci print worn over tights; artificial braids create fantastic hairdo. *Right:* 1965. Courrèges wool coatdress; twill bound with grosgrain ribbon; shovel hat.

PLATE 14. *Left:* 1966. Paco Rabanne plastic dress: gilded plastic rectangles joined by metal links. *Right:* 1966. Philippe Venet chiffon minidress: feather wig-hat.

PLATE 15. *Left:* 1966. Courrèges whipcord and organza jumpsuit: worn over flesh-colored underpants. *Right:* 1967. Mary Quant wool minidress: industrial zipper down the front; felt helmet with nylon braids.

PLATE 16. *Left:* 1967. Rudi Gernreich silk dress: loose, straight line; full dolman sleeves. *Right:* 1967. Bill Blass crepe wedding dress: silk crepe with coat with jewel buttons; ice-white stripes and scallops.

PLATE 17. *Left:* 1968. Oscar de la Renta organdy overblouse and shorts: floral appliqué (flowers punched and appliquéd with silver center); elasticized jersey shoe stocking by David Evins. *Right:* 1968. Anne Fogarty "little girl" dress: wig inspired by Little Orphan Annie.

PLATE 18. *Left:* 1968. Geoffrey Beene coatdress. *Right:* 1969. Cardin wool coat, hooded sweater and white skirt: coat falling to the instep, rimmed with black cording; ribbed sweater belted into short skirt.

PLATE 19. *Left:* 1969. Courrèges dress: curved dress with a carved-out V neckline. *Right:* 1969. Yves Saint Laurent evening dress: patchwork skirt of satin squares; blouse and scarf of sheer print.

PLATE 20. *Left:* 1970. Zandra Rhodes's quilted satin dress with a snakeskin choker hung with knotted suede strips. Worn with a fringed shawl and knee-high suede boots. *Right:* 1970. Crepe-de-chine dress with long georgette sleeves from the House of Dior. It is topped by a floor-length sheer sheath and worn with a tasseled turban and feather fan.

PLATE 21. *Left:* 1970. One of Saint Laurent's lamé "hooker" dresses. *Right:* 1971. Two silk semicircles by Chloé, one worn as a wraparound skirt, the other as a shawl; worn with a black jersey top.

PLATE 22. *Left:* 1971. Plaid wool pantsuit with matching tie and boy's billed cap; by Biba. *Right:* 1971. Tuffin and Foale's quilted trousers and checkerboard-print dress.

PLATE 23. *Left:* 1972. Bill Blass's nostalgic twenties-look ensemble with a drop-waisted top over a short, pleated skirt, a monogrammed scarf and a matching cloche. *Right:* 1972. Mary Quant's two-piece thirties-look polka-dot crepe-de-chine dress, worn with a crocheted turban and thick-soled sandals.

PLATE 24. *Left:* 1972. Bold fantasy-print cotton hostess dress from Horrockses. The sleeves feature the handkerchief hemline of the thirties. *Right:* 1973. Saint Laurent's thirties look features a wool-and-chenille velvet cardigan with an ostrich-feather collar, a pleated, wool-crepe skirt, a mousseline-de-soie blouse and a cloche.

PLATE 25. *Left:* 1973. This wool-jacketed suit by Ted Lapidus features a finger-length, bias-cut, flared jacket over bell-bottom trousers. *Right:* 1973. Roland Klein interprets the sensuous glamour of the thirties in this silk-jersey gown with tiny covered buttons down the front. The model wears a sleek turban and carries a leather envelope bag and a long faux fox-fur scarf.

PLATE 26. *Left:* 1974. More thirties-inspired glamour in Laug's pleated lamé top over a pleated crepe-georgette skirt. *Right:* 1974. Loris Azzare's version of the "Gatsby Look" in a mousseline-de-soie gown, worn over a crepe undersheath pailletted in pearls and colored paste gems.

PLATE 27. *Left:* 1974. This Sonia Rykiel cape has a ribbon-banded collar that crisscrosses the body and ties at the waist. The wool sweater, softly pleated skirt, scarf and felt slouch hat have a thirties "spy" look. *Right:* 1975. Wool-and-angora cape by Andre Peters, worn with a short shoulder cape and matching soft hat with scarf ties. The tweed trousers are by Wendy Dagworthy.

PLATE 28. *Left:* 1975. John Bates's ensemble with a nipped-waisted, dolman-sleeved duster over a dirndl-skirted shirtwaist dress. *Right:* 1975. Laura Ashley harked back to the era of Beatrix Potter for this pinafore worn over a cotton, floral-print, puff-sleeved blouse, and a cotton pin-tucked skirt. Over the pinafore is an apron.

PLATE 29. *Left:* 1976. Halston's classic crepe-de-chine shirtwaist dress and matching Ultrasuede jacket. *Right:* 1976. Saint Laurent's "rich peasant" look is exemplified by this billowing taffeta skirt, embroidered blouse and turban.

PLATE 30. *Left:* 1977. A flowered silk-chiffon strapless dinner dress with detachable full sleeves from Givenchy's Nouvelle Boutique. *Right:* 1977. A coordinated set of silk blouse, tie-on skirt and full-legged pants by Sisan for Valentino. A matching scarf is tied into a turban.

PLATE 31. *Left:* 1977. Kenzo's "Big Look" cotton shirt worn over a full-cut short skirt. *Right:* 1978. Courrèges's chevron-patterned cotton jacket trimmed with velvet, pullover sweater over man's shirt and ascot and cotton satin trousers. Worn with man-styled bluchers, a derby and a boutonniere.

PLATE 32. *Left:* 1978. This Mongolian-looking evening ensemble by Saint Laurent consists of a silk-cire hooded coat, embroidered with sequins and trimmed in mink, and satin pants trimmed with tassels, worn with mink-trimmed leather boots. Under the coat is a knitted gold jersey bodice. *Right:* 1978. Slinky, soft, narrow velvet dress with full-cut sleeves by Oscar de la Renta. The hammered brass belt is by Tess Shalom.

PLATE 33. *Left:* 1979. Thierry Mugler's creations were often outrageous, but strong on basic line, as in this space-age cotton jumpsuit. *Right:* 1979. Claude Montana exploits the new interest in wide shoulders in this gabardine trench coat.

PLATE 34. *Left:* 1979. Ralph Lauren redefines the classic man's smoking jacket in paisley silk trimmed in satin, putting it over a Victorian blouse and sleek trousers. *Right:* 1979. The bodice of this evening costume by Albert Caprero is of velvet trimmed with silk fringe. The shoulders and bosom are worked in jet beads and silk. The skirt is of the same ribbed silk.

PLATE 35. *Left:* 1980. Betty Hanson and Company shirt-waist dress and short jacket. Accessories include a belt, shoes, and hat with a handkerchief and bangle bracelet. *Right:* 1980. Missoni oversized, woolen plaid jacket and hat, worn with a box-pleated skirt. The red of the plaid is picked up in the heel of the shoes.

PLATE 36. *Left:* 1980. Claude Montana trousered, big cotton dress. *Right:* 1980. Classic sheath by Halston. The classic box coat is lapeled and lined.

PLATE 37. *Left:* 1981. Perry Ellis tank top with softly pleated skirt over flounced petticoats, with striped knit cap and stockings. *Right:* 1981. Calvin Klein oversized dress in a luxurious metallic print fabric. With a plunging neckline and wide leather belt, this dress was worn with knee-high leather boots.

PLATE 38. *Left:* 1982. Giorgio Armani layered blousson blouse with full cut-off pants. *Right:* 1982. Marc Bohan used black and white, a favorite Dior color theme, to create a suit with longer, narrower lines. It was accessorized with a black bow tie, earrings, gloves, and shoes.

PLATE 39. *Left:* 1982. Kasper silk tee shirt in graduated stripes, with belt, worn over a softly gathered long skirt in the same material. *Right:* 1983. Bernard Perris white flannel suit trimmed with snakeskin. Completing the ensemble was a broad pinwheel hat and large silk scarf worn in a puff at the shoulder.

PLATE 40. *Left:* 1983. Carolina Herrera's summer gown of striped and dotted organza has a fitted bodice and dirndl skirt. It was worn with a betsy, or ruff, at the neck.

Right: 1983. Karl Lagerfeld's luxurious dress with the image of a running faucet composed of beads and sequins. Designed for the House of Chloé, it may have been influenced by Schiaparelli's surrealist-informed designs of the thirties.

PLATE 41. *Left:* 1984. Bill Blass evening gown of heavy satin in lightning bolt colors. *Right:* 1984. Valentino evening sheath in silk jersey, the sparkling diamond clips emphasizing the squared shoulder line.

PLATE 42. *Left:* 1984. Norma Kamali fleece, man-styled topcoat worn with matching slacks, a super long scarf, and a brimmed hat reminiscent of a fedora. *Right:* 1985. Jacqueline de Ribes evening dress of silk crepe. It had a shaped, though non-confining, silhouette, and broad, rounded shoulders. De Ribes designed her own jewelry.

PLATE 43. *Left:* 1985. Donna Karan winter outfit combining a suede blousson jacket with broad, padded shoulders and an asymmetrical waistband. It was worn over a long, flared, wool jersey skirt and suede boots. *Right:* 1985. Gianfranco Ferré brightly colored suede jacket which was worn over full-cut slacks.

Plate 44. *Left:* 1986. Anne Klein broad-shouldered sweater dress featuring broad stripes of red, white, and black with a wide patent leather belt. *Right:* 1986. Adolfo dress with a full-length zipper from neck to hem. He's one of Nancy Reagan's favorite designers.

PLATE 45. *Left:* 1986. Krizia sweater dress and coat in a heavily ribbed cashmere and mohair blend. It was worn with a felt hat, shirt, gloves, and shoes. *Right:* 1987. Yves Saint Laurent evening dress of silk crepe with a plunging neckline, split skirt, and huge taffeta bow at the waist. It was accessorized with a cartwheel hat, long gloves, stockings, and shoes.

PLATE 46. *Left:* 1987. Geoffrey Beene layered, lace confection. *Right:* 1987. Oscar de la Renta shortened version of a fifties Dior dress with a touch of Schiaparelli's shocking pink.

Plate 47. *Left:* 1988. Arnold Scaasi evening gown with a low-cut, velvet bodice, a dropped waistline, and a billowing, satin skirt. *Right:* 1988. Emanuel Ungaro strapless bodice, dropped waist, over a full, shortened skirt, caught up to the side by a huge rose.

PLATE 48. *Left:* 1988. Lacroix two-piece zippered suit in wool with mink facing. Worn with a black bag and shoes. *Right:* 1988. Carolyn Roehm wool crepe dress topped with a bolero jacket.

PLATE 49. *Left:* 1989. Givenchy evening sheath severely tailored, covered with a flowing, full-length cape. *Right:* 1989. Bob Mackie classic evening gown in chiffon over magenta silk, worn with a sequin-studded spencer, or short jacket.

PLATE 50. *Left:* 1990. Emanuel Ungaro's lamé floral evening gown, simple but stunning in its cut and drape. *Right:* 1990. Christian Lacroix's silk print jacket and skirt ensemble cleverly mixes different patterns of the same color.

PLATE 51. *Left:* 1990. Geoffrey Beene's gold-dot silk jacquard evening ensemble with matching gloves. *Right:* 1991. Oscar de la Renta's gold silk shantung sleeveless dress with great coat.

PLATE 52. *Left:* 1991. Valentino's bell-skirted evening ensemble with sheer yoke and sleeves and bow accent. *Right:* 1991. A Todd Oldham patchwork plaid miniskirt suit with coordinated blouse.

PLATE 53. *Left:* 1992, Arnold Scaasi shows his mastery of the draper's craft in this polka dot strapless silk crepe dress. *Right:* 1992, Michael Kors' lace-over-silk short strapless dress, worn with coordinated cardigan.

PLATE 54. *Left:* 1992. Bob Mackie's dramatic evening gown with velvet top and silk taffeta skirt. *Right:* 1993. Simple knit tube dress achieves elegance in the hands of Bill Blass.

PLATE 55. *Left:* 1993. A Linda Allard for Ellen Tracy design: man-tailored bold pin-stripe suit with full trousers. *Right:* 1993. Adolfo's version of kabuki style in polka-dot prints, worn over matching bell bottoms.

PLATE 56. *Left:* 1994. Multi-tiered pleated silk gown marks a return to glamour by the House of Ricci. *Right:* 1994. Stunning high-contrast evening gown by Louis Féraud with huge, capelike collar.

PLATE 57. *Left:* 1994. Jean-Louis Scherrer combines the modern minidress with the classic ball gown in this embroidered, jeweled confection. *Right:* 1995. Gianfranco Ferré's classic bouclé suit and topcoat accented by oversized buttons.

PLATE 58. *Left:* 1995. Thierry Mugler's shaped, closely fitted wool miniskirted suit with flared jacket, worn over vinyl pants. *Right:* 1995. The name Vera Wang denotes memorable wedding dresses, but the designer is equally adept with elegant ball gowns, as displayed in this cyclamen-pink satin gown with corset-style bodice and voluminous net skirt and matching gloves.

PLATE 59. *Left:* 1996. Carolina Herrera's satin wedding suit; the lowcut jacket's coattails descend in a flared train. *Right:* 1996. Donna Karan's body-hugging silk knit dress in moss green.

PLATE 60. *Left:* 1996. Norma Kamali's panne velvet bolero with Mongolian lamb trim, worn over matching bell-bottom pants. *Right:* 1997. Isaac Mizrahi's tailored suit with plunging neckline reflects his love affair with bold color.

PLATE 61. *Left:* 1997. Giorgio Armani's unstructured great coat worn over soft, full-cut pants. *Right:* 1997. Gianni Versace's slinky silk knit evening gown in an innovative pairing of colors.

PLATE 62. *Left:* 1998. John Galliano's "Scheherazade" kimono and gown for Dior combine eastern motifs with Art Deco opulence. Silk velvet kimono worked with gold thread and gems; sheath dress is of double satin. *Right:* 1998. Karl Lagerfeld uses Meissen porcelain sequins to embellish this sheer black tulle dress for Chanel.

PLATE 63. *Left:* 1998. In spite of public protests and negative publicity, many designers continue to use fur. Here, Alexander McQueen for Givenchy presents a slim wool coat with enormous gray fox collar. *Right:* 1999. Ralph Lauren's evening separates combine a cropped cashmere turtleneck sweater with a dropped-waist satin ball skirt.

PLATE 64. *Left:* 1999. Revealing cotton-and-nylon beaded, lace-embroidered dress by Dolce & Gabbana. *Right:* 1999. Jean Paul Gaultier's "fan" design features a huge ostrich plume fan and beige silk gown with ostrich trim.

ABOUT THE DESIGNERS

Adolfo Sardina (b. 1933, Cuba) apprenticed to Balenciaga and then came to New York in 1948 as a millinery designer. In 1962 he started his own millinery business in New York. Switching to apparel design, he introduced a series of knits inspired by Chanel's famous tweed suits. *See Plates 44 and 55.*

Aldrich, Larry (1906–2001, United States) trained for the law, but began a career in fashion in 1927. Many of the fashions he featured, designed by Marie McCarthy, were French fashions adapted for the American woman. *See Plate 11.*

Allard, Linda (b. 1940, United States) studied fine arts at Kent State University. In New York, she designed for H. Gallen, who created the name "Ellen Tracy" as a vehicle to present Allard's designs for the well-dressed mainstream woman. *See Plate 55.*

Armani, Giorgio (b. 1934, Italy) studied medicine, philosophy, and worked as an assistant buyer at an Italian department store. His first menswear collection appeared in 1974, his womenswear collection in 1975. Pioneering the unconstructed blazer, Armani clothing has an easy fit, fine tailoring, and luxurious fabrics in neutral colors. *See Plates 38 and 61.*

Ashley, Laura (1926–1985, Wales) started her company in 1956 as a cottage industry, producing tea towels and table napkins before turning to fashion. *See Plate 28.*

Azzaro, Loris (b. 1934, Tunisia) taught French literature in his native country and in France before opening a shop in Paris in 1966 selling accessories and beaded evening tops. He soon became known for slinky evening wear. *See Plate 26.*

Balmain, Pierre (1914–1982, France). He studied to be an architect but financial reverses led to a career in Parisian couture. He worked for Molyneux and Lucien Lelong (with Dior) in the thirties and opened his own establishment in 1946. Not known for innovation, his creations are quietly luxurious and his clientele the aristocrats of world society. *See Plate 8.*

Bates, John (b. 1938, England) worked for Herbert Sidon, 1956–58. He became the chief designer for Jean Varon, 1961. In 1974 he launched a line using his own name. *See Plate 28.*

Beene, Geoffrey (b. 1927, United States). A medical student before studying fashion design in New York City, he joined Teal Traina in 1958. Opening his own business in 1962, he is known for his imaginative use of color and for the wearability of his clothing. *See Plates 18, 46, and 51.*

Biba. Influential London boutique opened in 1963, the brainchild of fashion illustrator and designer Barbara Hulanicki. In 1969, Biba took over an Art Deco building in Kensington High Street. *See Plate 22.*

Blass, Bill (b. 1922, United States) started as a sketch artist in New York, served in the army in WWII, then joined Anna Miller, Ltd., in 1946. He stayed with the firm when it merged with Maurice Rentner in 1959, becoming vice president, then owner. In 1970, the firm became Bill Blass, Ltd. His womenswear designs mix exquisite menswear fabrics, patterns and textures. He has been a mentor to many young American designers. *See Plates 16, 23, 41, and 54.*

Bohan, Marc (b. 1926, France) worked for Robert Piguet and Jean Patou before joining the House of Dior in 1958. He took over its leadership in 1960, replacing Yves Saint Laurent. Marc Bohan designs are known for soft prints, ruffles, pleats, and embroidery. *See Plate 38.*

Caprero, Albert (b. 1943, United States) worked for Lily Daché and Oscar de la Renta before forming a company with Ben Shaw and Jerry Guttenberg. In 1975, he gained fame when First Lady Betty Ford chose his clothes for her spring wardrobe. *See Plate 34.*

Capucci, Roberto (b. 1929, Italy). Working in Italy from the end of World War II, Capucci moved his base to Paris in 1962, but returned to Rome six years later. His work is marked by the use of nontraditional materials and experimental cut. *See Plate 8.*

Cardin, Pierre (b. 1922, Italy) grew up in St.-Etienne, France. He worked with Paquin and Castillo; then helped Dior create "new look." In 1950 he opened his own business, called Adam and Eve, which sold women's dresses and some accessories for men. He opened his design house in 1957. He was the first designer to present both men's and women's fashions together, sparking the unisex idea. *See Plate 18.*

Chanel, Gabrielle "Coco" (1883–1971, France). A dominant figure in fashion from the mid-twenties; she closed her design house at the occupation of France in 1940. At age 71 in 1954 she reopened her couture house to almost immediate success. *See Plates 11 and 62.*

Chloé. Upscale French ready-to-wear house founded in 1952. The principal designers for the firm in 1971 were Karl Lagerfeld and Graziella Fontana. *See Plates 21 and 40.*

Courrèges, André (b. 1923, France). After a long association with Balenciaga, he opened his own house in 1961. He was one of the leading innovators of the sixties, introducing the miniskirt and trouser suit. He closed his couture business in 1966, reopening with three different divisions, each catering to a different price group. *See Plates 9, 12, 13, 15, 19, and 31.*

Dagworthy, Wendy (b. 1950, England) designed for a wholesale firm before opening her own company in 1972. In 1975, she joined the London Designer Collections, a designer's cooperative. *See Plate 27.*

de la Renta, Oscar (b. 1932, Dominican Republic) worked for Balenciaga in Madrid, then moved to Paris in 1961 as assistant to Antonio de Castillo. In 1963 he went to New York to design at Elizabeth Arden. He joined Jane Derby in 1965; the firm began operating as Oscar de la Renta, Ltd. after her death. De la Renta designs are extravagantly romantic and sophisticated. *See Plates 17, 32, 46, and 51.*

de Ribes, Jacqueline (b. 1930, France). An international society figure renowned for her elegant personal style, Comtesse de Ribes was once dubbed "the most stylish woman in the world" by *Town & Country* magazine. Her first show was in 1982. De Ribes's fashions are known for their aristocratic look of discreet grandeur and slender lines. She is also recognized for her outstanding jewelry design. *See Plate 42.*

Dior, Christian (1905–1957, France) opened his own house in 1947, launching "New Look," a world-shattering collection of luxurious fashions. After Dior's death in 1957, his place was taken by his protégé, Yves Saint Laurent, whose association with the house ended when he was drafted in 1960. Marc Bohan then directed the house. *See Plates 5, 20, 38, and 62.*

Dolce & Gabbana. Domenico Dolce (b. 1958, Italy) and Stefano Gabbana (b. 1962, Italy) met in Milan and held their first solo womenswear show in 1986. Their popularity soared when Madonna endorsed one of their shirts in her movie *Truth or Dare.* The duo is famous for celebrating the curvaceous female form in their designs. *See Plate 64.*

Ellis, Perry (1940–1986, United States). After working as a sportswear buyer, American Perry Ellis began to design for the Portfolio Division of Vera Industries in 1975. Perry Ellis Sportswear, Inc. was established in 1978; Perry Ellis Menswear in 1980. His designs were known for their youth, spirit, and natural fabrics. *See Plate 37.*

Ferré, Gianfranco (b. 1945, Italy). After early starts in architecture and jewelry and accessory design, he opened his own couture house in 1974. His fine tailoring reflects his background in architecture. *See Plates 43 and 57.*

Fogarty, Anne (1919–1981, United States). A former model, she became famous for her paper-doll silhouette. *See Plate 17.*

Féraud, Louis (1920–1999, France). In 1955 Féraud opened a boutique in Cannes. His first great success was a dress for Brigitte Bardot. His clothing blends simple structure with graphic detailing. *See Plate 56.*

Galitzine, Irene (Princess) (b. ca. 1916, Russia). Her aristocratic family fled to Italy from the Russian Revolution, where she studied art. Based in Rome, she worked for three years for the Fontana sisters and presented her first collection in 1949. *See Plate 7.*

Galliano, John (b. 1960, Spain). Inspired by Madeleine Vionnet and Paul Poiret, Galliano is the master of the bias cut. First professional collection presented under his own name in October 1984. *See Plate 62.*

Gaultier, Jean Paul (b. 1952, France). At 17 he was hired by Pierre Cardin as a design assistant. Gaultier went out on his own in 1976. His witty styles always challenge the Paris establishment. *See Plate 64.*

Gernreich, Rudi (1922–1985, Austria). Operating out of Los Angeles, he won renown as a pioneer of the miniskirt and the creator of the topless bathing suit. *See Plate 16.*

Givenchy, Hubert de (b. 1927, France) began his career at age 17 working for Jacques Fath, later moving to Piguet and Schiaparelli. He opened his own house in 1952 with a collection of inexpensive cottons, and was a smash success. His later couture was greatly influenced by his friend and master, Balenciaga. Givenchy's clothing is revered for its elegant cut, fabric and workmanship. *See Plates 9, 30, 49, and 63.*

Griffe, Jacques (b. 1917, France). Having spent three years with Vionnet, he became a master of construction, especially in handling the bias cut; established a boutique and ready-to-wear range. *See Plate 7.*

Halston (1932–1990, United States) started as a millinery designer, working for Lily Daché and Bergdorf Goodman. Halston originated the pillbox hat made famous by Jackie Kennedy in 1961 at the Kennedy inauguration. He began designing ready-to-wear in the late sixties, opening his own firm in 1972. In 1973, he sold the business to Norton Simon. *See Plates 11, 29, and 36.*

Hanson, Betty and Company. Formed in 1976, Betty Hanson and Company was a family-run business; Hall and Steven Hanson directed the operations. With imaginative use of texture, fabric, color, and shape, their clothing was intended for "real-life" dressing. *See Plate 35.*

Heim, Jacques (1899–1967, France). The son of furriers, Heim was one of the first designers to sense the coming of the youth-oriented fashion era. The House of Heim closed, 1969; later reopened by new organization that purchased name. *See Plate 5.*

Herrera, Carolina (b. 1939, Venezuela) experienced the world of high society and couture clothes growing up in Caracas, Venezuela. She launched her first ready-to-wear collection in 1981, focusing on elegant day and evening wear. Her chic designs drew a following that included Jacqueline Onassis, Nancy Reagan, and Caroline Kennedy. *See Plates 40 and 59.*

Horrockses. British ready-to-wear firm specializing in sophisticated cotton fashions. *See Plate 24.*

Hulanicki, Barbara (b. 1938, Poland). See Biba.

Kamali, Norma (b. 1945, United States) studied fashion illustration at the Fashion Institute of Technology. In 1969, she and her husband, Eddie Kamali, opened a tiny shop selling British imports and her inventive designs. Moving to Madison Avenue in 1974, she designed suits and lace dresses. In 1977, divorced, she established a new boutique and company called OMO (On My Own). *See Plates 42 and 60.*

Karan, Donna (b. 1948, United States) is the daughter of a fashion model and a haberdasher. After attending the Parsons School of Design for two years, she left to work under Anne Klein, and after Klein's death in 1974, became co-designer with Parsons classmate Louis Dell'Olio. In 1984 she opened her own firm. Her designs offer practical, flattering wearability. *See Plates 43 and 59.*

Kasper, Herbert (b. 1926, United States). Beginning as a hat designer, in 1985 American Herbert Kasper opened a sportswear company respected for its tailored, sophisticated clothing. *See Plate 39.*

Kenzo (b. 1940, Japan). Moved to Paris in the mid-sixties. After designing several freelance collections, he opened his first boutique, Jungle Jap, in 1970. *See Plate 31.*

Klein, Anne (1923–1974, United States) was the founder of the Junior Sophisticates label, where she pioneered sophisticated styles for women 5'4" tall and under. In 1968 she established Anne Klein & Co. Her sportswear was well-suited to the American woman's lifestyle. *See Plate 44.*

Klein, Calvin (b. 1942, United States). Calvin Klein, Ltd., established in 1968, is revered for its understated, refined, luxurious fabrics. *See Plate 37.*

Klein, Roland (b. 1938, France) worked for Dior and Patou in Paris before moving to England in 1965. In London, he worked at Marcel Fenez, where he had his own label. He opened his own ready-to-wear business in 1979. *See Plate 25.*

Kors, Michael (b. 1959, United States) briefly attended the Fashion Institute of Technology; he left to learn about fashion first-hand at a New York boutique. He opened his design house in 1981 and is known for his sophisticated designer sportswear. *See Plate 53.*

Krizia (Kriziamaglia, a company, Italy). Founded by Mariuccia Mandelli in 1952, Krizia clothing is refined and witty. *See Plate 45.*

Lacroix, Christian (b. 1951, France). A museum curator before becoming a designer, he opened his own couture and ready-to-wear business in mid-1987. He has been credited with revitalizing Paris couture with his irreverent wit and imaginative designs. *See Plates 48 and 50.*

Lagerfeld, Karl (b. 1939, Germany). The sole designer at Chloé in 1972, in 1984 he created his own label at Chanel, designing a sportswear collection specifically for the United States market in 1985. *See Plates 40 and 62.*

Lapidus, Ted (1929, France) studied technology in Tokyo; returned to Paris in his early twenties and opened a small dressmaking house. He also designed for several ready-to-wear manufacturers. *See Plate 25.*

Laug, André (b. 1932, France) worked for Nina Ricci and André Courrèges, then moved to Italy where he designed for Antonelli. He opened his own couture house in 1968 and also produced ready-to-wear. *See Plate 26.*

Lauren, Ralph (b. 1939, United States) began his career in fashion retailing. In 1968, he began designing a line of menswear under the label "Polo by Ralph Lauren," then branched into women's clothing in 1971. He is known for his representation of an idealized American past in his high-quality fashions, which exude an air of privileged luxury. *See Plates 34 and 63.*

Mackie, Bob (b. 1940, United States). He studied art and theater design and worked as a sketcher for film designers such as Edith Head. In 1969 he opened his own salon and made a splash with glamorous ready-to-wear evening clothes. *See Plates 49 and 54.*

McQueen, Alexander (b. 1969, England). Considered an "enfant terrible" of the fashion world, McQueen graduated from Central Saint Martin's College of Art and Design in 1992 and quickly gained a reputation as an iconoclast. In March 1994, he formed his own label and in 1996 he took over from John Galliano at the House of Givenchy. *See Plate 63.*

Missoni, Rosita and Ottavio (Tai) (Italy). Opening their business in 1953 with four knitting machines, Rosita designed elegant garments while Tai created inventively colored knit patterns. *See Plate 35.*

Mizrahi, Isaac (b. 1961, United States). He studied at New York's High School of Performing Arts and the Parsons School of Design. His trademark is an unusual, even, comic mix of vibrant color with an easy-to-wear, traditional cut. *See Plate 60.*

Montana, Claude (b. 1949, France) began designing papier-mâché jewelry in London in 1971. He stayed in London for a year, then returned to Paris, where he worked for the leather firm MacDouglas and designed for several ready-to-wear firms. In 1979 he established his own business creating clothing with bold, defined shapes. *See Plates 33 and 36.*

Mugler, Thierry (b. 1946, France) showed his first collection in Paris in 1971 under the label Café de Paris; by 1973, he was showing clothes under his own name. *See Plates 33 and 58.*

Oldham, Todd (b. 1961, United States) is known for his bold use of color and for serving up kitschy styles with panache. *See Plate 52.*

Patou, Jean (House of): originally creating fashions that were quintessential "Jazz Age," the house hired Karl Lagerfeld in 1960. *See Plate 10.*

Perris, Bernard (b. 1944, France). With early training that included assisting Marc Bohan at Dior, Bernard Perris established a ready-to-wear firm in 1969. His couture-centered designs have a youthful spirit. *See Plate 39.*

Pucci, Emilio (b. 1914–1992, Italy), one of the earliest designers to establish an Italian influence in the postwar era; noted for his printed fabrics. *See Plate 13.*

Quant, Mary (b. 1934, England), a leading figure in the fashion revolution of the sixties, she opened her first boutique in 1955. In 1967, she opened the wildly successful boutique Bazaar on King's Road, 1967; featuring mass-produced miniskirts and fashions that had powerful appeal to the young. *See Plates 15 and 23.*

Rabanne, Paco (b. 1934, Spain) opened his Paris house in 1966. His designs are created through "molding and welding." *See Plate 14.*

Rhodes, Zandra (b. 1940, England) began her career as a textile designer in the mid-sixties, setting up her own printworks with a partner. She began designing clothes using her own fabrics, and, by 1969, was working on her own. Zandra Rhodes Limited was established in 1975. *See Plate 20.*

Ricci, Nina (1883–1970, Italy). At age 13 she was apprenticed to a couturier, and by 21 she was a top stylist. In 1932 she opened her own house, specializing in elegant women's clothes. She was noted for intensely feminine fashions and was one of the first to realize the potential of ready-to-wear. Her principal designer was Jules-François Grahay from 1954–63, followed by Gérard Pipart. *See Plates 6 and 56.*

Roehm, Carolyn (b. 1951, United States). She was an assistant designer at Oscar de la Renta, Ltd. from 1975 to 1984, opening Carolyn Roehm Inc. in 1984. Her garments are made in luxurious, embroidered fabrics. *See Plate 48.*

Rykiel, Sonia (b. 1930, France) began her career in 1962 designing her own maternity sweaters. She continued designing after the birth of her child, selling her designs first through her husband's Paris boutique, then through Galeries Lafayette. In 1968, she opened her own store on Paris's Left Bank. *See Plate 27.*

Saint Laurent, Yves (b. 1936, Algeria). Heading the House of Dior after Dior's death in 1957, he opened his own design house in 1962 and Rive Gauche ready-to-wear boutiques in 1966. Saint Laurent popularized blazers, city pants, military jackets, simple dresses divided into Mondrian-inspired blocks of color, and many other styles. In 1963 he became the first living designer to be given a retrospective of his work at New York's Metropolitan Museum of Art. *See Plates 6, 10, 12, 19, 21, 24, 29, 32, and 45.*

Scaasi, Arnold (b. 1931, Canada). He trained with Charles James, leaving in 1957 to establish his own business. Originally a sketcher and wholesaler, he presented his first ready-to-wear collection in 1960. His specialty is eye-catching evening clothes and spectacular society ball gowns. *See Plates 47 and 53.*

Scherrer, Jean-Louis (b. 1936, France). His early dance career ended with an injury. He then worked for Christian Dior. After Dior's death, Scherrer opened his own house in 1962. His elegant designs reflect his couture background. *See Plate 57.*

Tuffin and Foale. Sally Tuffin (b. 1938, England) and Marion Foale (b. 1939, England) set up a dressmaking business in 1961. Based on Carnaby Street, their designs were aimed at the young ready-to-wear market. The partnership was dissolved in 1972. *See Plate 22.*

Ungaro, Emanuel (b. 1933, France) became a tailor at the age of 14. He first worked for Balenciaga, then Courrèges; in 1965 he opened his own establishment. In the sixties Ungaro was known for his short, structured dresses in bold stripes or plaids and hip-hugger pants.

By the seventies he was showing softer colors, shapes, and fabrics. His designs have since become more revealing and sensuous. *See Plates 47 and 50.*

Valentino, (b. 1933, Italy) has been called the "master of the dress." He studied fashion at the Chambre Syndicale de la Couture. He opened his own design house in Rome in 1959 and his first boutique in Milan in 1969, with many boutiques to follow. Valentino has created gowns for international socialites; Jacqueline Onassis was a client. *See Plates 30, 41, and 52.*

Venet, Philippe (b. 1929, France) worked with Schiaparelli and Givenchy before opening his own house in 1962. His fashions feature elegance of cut. *See Plate 14.*

Versace, Gianni (1946–1997, Italy). Versace's mother was a dressmaker, and he was surrounded by fashion from childhood. He studied architecture but became increasingly involved in his mother's couture business. From rock stars to royalty, his bold, flamboyant designs were worn by men and women in the public eye. His sister, Donatella, carries on the line. *See Plate 61.*

Wang, Vera (b. 1949, United States). Through her acquaintance with Ralph Lauren, Wang opened a bridal salon and couture business in 1990. Her use of rich fabric, surface decoration, and netting are masterful and dramatic. *See Plate 58.*

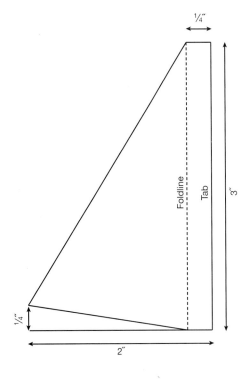

NOTE

To stand the dolls, fold the white part of the bases back. Using a lightweight cardboard (such as oaktag), cut a brace for each doll, following the diagram. Fold each brace along the foldline indicated in the diagram to form a tab. Center the tab on the back of the doll with the lower edge even with the fold in the base; glue in place.